IT'S TIME TO EAT GUAVA

It's Time to Eat GUAVA

Walter the Educator

Silent King Books
A WhichHead Entertainment Imprint

Copyright © 2024 by Walter the Educator

All rights reserved. No part of this book may be reproduced in any manner whatsoever without written per- mission except in the case of brief quotations embodied in critical articles and reviews.

First Printing, 2024

Disclaimer

This book is a literary work; the story is not about specific persons, locations, situations, and/or circumstances unless mentioned in a historical context. Any resemblance to real persons, locations, situations, and/or circumstances is coincidental. This book is for entertainment and informational purposes only. The author and publisher offer this information without warranties expressed or implied. No matter the grounds, neither the author nor the publisher will be accountable for any losses, injuries, or other damages caused by the reader's use of this book. The use of this book acknowledges an understanding and acceptance of this disclaimer.

It's Time to Eat GUAVA is a collectible early learning book by Walter the Educator suitable for all ages belonging to Walter the Educator's Time to Eat Book Series. Collect more books at WaltertheEducator.com

USE THE EXTRA SPACE TO TAKE NOTES AND DOCUMENT YOUR MEMORIES

GUAVA

It's time to eat, come gather 'round,

It's Time to Eat Guava

A guava treat is what we've found!

Green or yellow, round and sweet,

Oh, what a lovely fruit to eat!

Slice it open, what's inside?

Pink or white, it's such a surprise!

Tiny seeds and juicy bliss,

A guava's taste is not to miss!

Take a sniff, oh what a smell,

A fruity scent we know so well.

Fresh and fragrant, it's such a delight,

Guava's magic feels just right.

Crunchy bites or soft and smooth,

It's a fruit that fits your mood.

Sweet like candy, bright and bold,

A treasure worth its weight in gold.

It's Time to Eat
Guava

Eat it plain or make some juice,

Guava's good for many use.

A healthy snack, it's full of cheer,

With guava, smiles are always near.

Packed with vitamins, A and C,

It's good for you, it's plain to see!

Strong and happy you'll surely grow,

Guava's the secret, now you know!

From sunny trees it loves to grow,

In warm, bright places, just so you know.

A fruit from nature, fresh and free,

It's guava time for you and me!

So grab a guava, take a bite,

Morning, noon, or late at night.

It's tasty, healthy, fun to eat,

A guava's goodness can't be beat!

One for me, and one for you,

Let's share this fruit with all we do.

Guava time is here to stay,

A yummy treat to brighten the day!

It's Time to Eat
Guava

Now that you know, go spread the cheer,

Tell everyone, both far and near.

Guava fruit is pure delight,

Let's have some more starting tonight!

ABOUT THE CREATOR

Walter the Educator is one of the pseudonyms for Walter Anderson. Formally educated in Chemistry, Business, and Education, he is an educator, an author, a diverse entrepreneur, and he is the son of a disabled war veteran. "Walter the Educator" shares his time between educating and creating. He holds interests and owns several creative projects that entertain, enlighten, enhance, and educate, hoping to inspire and motivate you. Follow, find new works, and stay up to date with Walter the Educator™

at WaltertheEducator.com

www.ingramcontent.com/pod-product-compliance
Lightning Source LLC
LaVergne TN
LVHW052012060526
838201LV00059B/3997